Daring to be Different

Daring to be Different

✦

25 Tips for A Life of Success

Darrell Bennett, Jr. A Morehouse College Student

iUniverse, Inc.
New York Lincoln Shanghai

Daring to be Different
25 Tips for A Life of Success

iUniverse, Inc.

For information address:
iUniverse, Inc.
2021 Pine Lake Road, Suite 100
Lincoln, NE 68512
www.iuniverse.com

ISBN: 0-595-32459-2

Printed in the United States of America

I would like to dedicate this book to my Lord and Saviour,
who has given me life,
and my mother, Wanda Clarke, who has always been there
to guide me through it.

If you would like to contact the author, please feel free to do so.
Jaybenjr@aol.com
www.DarrellBennett.com

Fletch & Scout:

I hope you
enjoy this!

Contents

25 Tips for Life of Success

Dear Reader:

I congratulate you on your decision to become successful. This is the first step in a process that will last your entire life. Before you go any further you must make up your mind that you can and you will do what it takes to transform your life. As you read this book you will notice that I include the word successful a number of times. Who determines success? You do. Each person has a niche and a purpose on this earth that will help make their society a better place. Success is merely the most efficient path to achieving that purpose. Success is not one goal or one event; it is a lifestyle, the manner of your very being.

Have I achieved success? I wish. I am an 18 year old junior at Morehouse College and like you, striving to be a better person. This book is merely my way of giving back to our society, which has given me so much. I discuss what I think success is—the good, the bad, the ugly—and how best to travel on this lonely road. I wrote this especially for those like me, the young aspiring individual, but I encourage people of all ages to share it. I believe I have enclosed a wealth of advice; my only hope is that you benefit from it.

Get your highlighter and notepad. Sit back, relax, and enjoy.

Sincerely,
Darrell Bennett, Jr.

25 Tips for Life of Success

1.

Demand Excellence of Yourself

This is the first and foremost rule. In order to be successful in anything in life, you must demand excellence of yourself. Do not simply ask or suggest it—*demand* your absolute best. I say demand it because it is essential in order to gear you mentally for the tough road ahead. I did not think until I got to college that I was a perfectionist. As a matter of a fact I tried to shun the title because of its negative connotation, but soon enough I had to come to grips with myself and that I was indeed a perfectionist. I adopted the attitude from my mother, who never applauded anything less than excellence. A's were praised; B's were tolerated, and anything else, well, they did not happen.

This principle made all the difference in my life. I graduated with the IB diploma in June 2003; perhaps I should add that I was the only black male in my city to do so that year. I went on the Morehouse College where I fought tooth and nail for the highest grades possible. I realize that in pushing myself to excel I am producing a work ethic that will last much longer than the grades on my report card. I encourage you to do the same. Work hard, and work diligently. Do the best you can, the first time around. Aim to impress those around you and you will.

The alternative is hopelessness. I had a friend in high school that never applied himself. It was as if he tried to do just the bare minimum. He always seemed to slip by classes with C's and low B's, partly because he seemed to fail so many tests because he didn't study and partly because he never had much to contribute to class conversations. He never did any sports or even any extracurricular activities. Even on the SATs, of which he knew the importance full well before he took them, he went in unrehearsed, not even bothering to take a practice test. His score was so low that it prompted another of my friend's dads to ask whether he had *combined* the math and verbal scores—ha-ha-ha. His overall attitude toward everything in life can be described as sloppy at best because his carelessness permeated his very existence.

Excellence shows itself through us in two ways: our results or work ethic, which we talked about, and our personality. Demanding excellence of your personality means that you are the first you look to for improvement. In other words when there is a problem, instead of finding fault in everyone else around you, you look internally. You should be the first to recognize and reform your inner self. Do not wait for someone else to point it out. Striving for success simply means you are a work in progress. A relative once told me that the people you see on the way up are the same people you see on the way down. That simply means be nice to others, not only because that may be beneficial to you in the long run, but because it's the civil thing to do. Exhibit humility and temperance. Always show respect where respect is due. The age-old adage "treat others like you want to be treated yourself", really says it all.

2.
Pick Your Company

Forget what you eat; you are what you hang around with. Those who are closest to you have a tendency to rub off on you. Their characteristics and mannerisms soon become yours. Trust me, I know. Since coming to college I made many acquaintances (and notice I say acquaintances) that I might not have otherwise. Call it luck, fate or intuition. I simply call it dorm assignments. Naturally I spent most of my time with the people in my dorm and on my floor, and I began to pick up their habits. I remember one guy in particular had this saying with which he prefaced almost every thought, and low and behold, soon enough everybody on the floor was repeating it.

I was told all my life by teachers and counselors and even TV programs that cliques are a middle and high school thing and that once one becomes an adult that whole idea becomes quite childish. Wrong!! I cannot stress enough that in college not only are there more cliques but they are even more exclusive, and if you go to college you know what I am talking about. I mean it's ridiculous. You've got the fraternities and then the interests of the fraternities. You've got the sports' teams and then the sports' team "groupies". You've got the SGA and the people "about to be" in the SGA. Then there are the "partiers", "the smokers", and then the "lame ones". The rest of the student population, well, they are not even worth being mentioned. I was blown away. If Morehouse, an all male HBCU, can be so diverse, then I could just imagine how a typical college or university is.

It is almost impossible not to become part of a certain group. I guess if I had to pick a group that I am associated with in college, it would be the "cool people". Ha-ha-ha—I wish. I was somebody who tried to jump from clique to clique until I realized that I was becoming more alienated. As my second semester rolled around I made it a point to become close to people I thought I had a lot to learn from. It worked because I sure learned a lot, but the stigma that followed was not so great. They called us arrogant and conceited but like anything in life one must weigh the positives against the negatives. And I say that it was worth it, because what I gained sure outweighed some of the negative things said about us.

To you I say do the same. Take a long look at the people you hang around with and ask yourself what it is about them that you like. (Stuff like "funny" and "easy-going" are gimmes.) If you cannot find a positive trait in them that you would like to have, then they are probably doing you more harm than good. Don't be fooled into thinking that you can hang out with a despicable person and not in time become despicable yourself. Does this mean that you cannot hang out with anyone that is not perfect? Absolutely not. Nobody is perfect; everyone has flaws, some though have much more than others. It only means that you have to choose how close you become to this person. (I talk more about that in the next section.) It really is serious; sometimes the difference between the White House and the Big House all depends on the type of people with whom you choose to hang around and which characteristics of theirs rub off on you.

3.
Cherish Your Friendships

No; it is not true that the more popular you are, the more friends you will have. You might have more acquaintances and more fans, but you will not have more friends. I was as popular as one can be in high school and I still only had a handful of friends. As a matter of fact being popular made it harder to have friends, (but that's a different conversation).

I call them a few good men—and women. They are your support system. They are your anchors. They are there for you when nobody else is. Everyone needs them but few have them. They are essential to one's development as a successful individual because they are the only ones with whom you can share your innermost thoughts and ideas without fear of being criticized or condemned.

My best friend is a guy I met in high school and who I now call my brother. I learned a lot from him about how to be a better person. I used to think he was quiet because he was weird, ha-ha. But soon I figured out that he was quiet because I was talking too much. As we became friends I realized that he had a lot to say and what he said I'll never forget. Please believe me, we fought and I didn't like how he would tell me about myself when I didn't want to hear it, but I am truly a better person for it now.

In college I met several people about whom I can say I will be life-long friends. A pre-med major on the third floor of my dorm was the one who helped me through the treacherous first semester. He is very determined and when I became tired of studying, he was there. I do not think he ever realized it, but just by being around him I became more focused, because I figured that as long as I at least stayed with him, I would be OK. Another of my friends is on the other side of my floor. I met him at a program at UPenn's Wharton in June 2002 and this past year we became even closer. We do not see eye-to-eye much. OK, we rarely saw eye-to-eye, but he is a loyal guy. He was there during both of my elections, and he never gave up hope. These two girls over at Spelman are among those I call friends. During my campaign they continued to campaign for me and anytime I wanted to hang out, they were there. They really helped me through some very hard times. Of course, I can't forget my boy, my partner in crime. I met him the first week of school and I thought we were like night and day. He managed my campaigns and was always there when I needed him. He taught me the meaning of loyalty. Even when so many others said all kinds of negative stuff about me, he continued to back me. Of everyone I met in college I am most thankful to have him as a friend.

Make friends. Cherish them and never let go. It is important to remember that a friend should be able to do more than just make you laugh. A friend should be trustworthy, meaning that if you would not leave him/her in your room alone then he/she cannot be trusted. A friend should be able to point out your mistakes constructively and praise your achievements. To answer the gender question, I say yes. Yes, a male can have a female friend and vice versa. Loyalty, honesty, good-heartedness are not gender traits—they are human traits.

Of course like anything else there are telltale signs of non-friends. Someone always criticizing your shortcomings and failures is *not* a friend. Someone who goes along with what people say to avoid being associated with you is *not* a friend. Someone who tells everyone all your business and secrets is a *not* a friend. But most of all, someone who is only hanging around with you to get something is *not* a friend.

4.
The Haters

These are my favorite people. They are always around and they are always talking—negatively that is. They say things like: "Who does she think she is?", "Why did they pick him?", "Don't let it go to your head.", "Well, it's not such a big deal.", and of course "I could have gotten it too, if I really wanted it." They are part parasitic, because they try to suck the life out of their victims, and part scavenger, because they flock around when one is at his/her lowest. But they can be seen as a benefit. When you have them, you must be doing something big.

I have always had them. They said I was "too white" in grade school, "too ambitious" in high school, and "too arrogant" now in college. I wish I could say that I always ignored them. I couldn't. The more I tried to be good at what I did, the more they seemed to surface. This is the same phenomenon that causes so many children to think that it is "cool" to be dumb. In middle school, I knew a guy who was extremely intelligent but would not answer the questions posed to him by the teacher. Finally I asked him why he played dumb and he told me he had a "rep[utation]" to uphold. (Today, he is in jail.) My mother would have none of that. She told me to thank God that I was different and celebrate my uniqueness, not shun it. I wish I could say that college was better, but it was not. After only one semester at college, people said I was too competitive and too aggressive and some hated me for it. In retrospect I guess I gave them a few reasons. I came in with 27 credits from high school. I had a full scholarship. I was ranked #1 in my class. I was a Bonner's Scholar. I had eaten dinner with a former African president and had spoken with two US Presidential candidates. I met Oprah Winfrey. Then on top of it all, I was selected along with 6 others from my class to be Man of the Year. Maybe that's why when I ran for class president someone looked at me and sneered, "I guess you want it all, don't you?"

Being hated will get you down and make you wonder why on earth you should continue trying to be successful. You will be dismayed and even become a bit ashamed of your accomplishments. These feelings are only normal, but just don't let them last long. There is another way to look at it. It's like having a fan club; they can always be counted on to tell everyone of your latest accomplishment, even if it is through sarcasm.

If you are one of the people that I just described—hated on for being successful—then I have a few words of advice. First of all, realize this. Haters will *never* embrace you for who you are. Haters will *never* appreciate your talents. Haters will *always* find something bad to say. So having said that, this is what you do. Forget them. Yup, there I said it. Forget those lame, good-for-nothing vultures. Let them talk; in fact give them more to talk about. If they hate your grades; make them higher. If they hate your clothes; walk around like a model. If they hate your speech; learn better vocabulary. Never ever let it appear in public that they are getting to you. And finally, be happy that you have a group of people who have so graciously devoted their lives to making yours seem much more glamorous than it actually is.

5.
Never Let Them See You Sweat

My mother always told me this, but I never really knew what it meant until this past year. College, among many other things, is a big pressure-cooker. It seems as if everything is bearing down on you at once. At times I felt as if everything that could go wrong for that week had already gone wrong, and it was only Thursday. But it was at times like these that this principle became of optimal importance.

Poised. Calm. Collective. These are all traits that I have learned in my short time away from home that one must possess in order to succeed. You must especially exhibit these characteristics in public. In order words, you can be as emotional as you want to be, but when you are in public and in the open, never let them see you sweat. There is something unique about a person who appears as if everything is always going great. That's when the poker face comes in handy. You can be tearing up inside, but when it counts you have to appear as if things could never be better. Does this mean you always have to smile? No, not if you do not normally. You should act as if everything is just fine without missing a beat. Does this mean never express your true feelings? Absolutely not. When you are with friends and loved ones feel free to show how you really feel. Does being this way mean you are being fake? No. Everybody has many sides and chooses which to let everyone else see. The fact is that your personal tragedies and circumstances are nobody's business, but going around looking pathetic only makes it that way. In addition, those haters that we were talking about before would love nothing more than to see that what they say about you is getting the best of you.

My point is that by applying this principle, you present yourself to the world as a person of poise and balance, who does not take everything to heart. By doing this, one is also inclined to think that it takes more than silly antics or vicious pranks to get you down. This, in turn, will win you respect—yes, even from those haters. I know this first-hand. I lost not one, but two elections for class president by about 5% of the vote each time. I cried and pouted and complained and even sulked—but never once in public. I smiled after the elections just as I had before. People would never know that it literally pained me to smile, because

I would not give them a reason to. Someone said to me later on: "It's quite ironic, no matter what people say about you, you just keep on smiling and you don't let it get to you." Ha-ha. Little did he know.

6.
It's OK to Envy. It's Jealousy that's the Problem

Some psychologists say that it is unhealthy to be envious of others. I could not disagree more. It is normal and quite good to envy. I think it is what gives one the fuel to drive one's ambitions. We envy others for their looks, their body, their accomplishments, their fame or their power. But the problem comes when it turns into jealousy.

I guess you can look at it like Envy being the brother of Jealousy. Jealousy snides, "How come she got picked?" while Envy asks, "How can I be picked too?" Jealousy mocks; Envy imitates. My high school friend, who happened to be a cheerleader, always says, "Don't hate, appreciate." I know it's corny, but it can make all the difference. If you want something someone else has, find out how they got it and work hard for it as well. Had the young Octavian been jealous of his uncle's power and tried to tear him down instead of following behind him and learning his art, he probably would have not grown to become the most celebrated emperor in Roman history, Caesar Augustus. Just as if Cain had bothered to learn why Abel's offering was accepted and his not, maybe he would not have brutally murdered him. History is polluted with examples of how the thin line between envy and jealousy has written the course of human existence.

Does this mean that you want to be someone else? No. You appreciate who you are but you do find a trait in someone else that you wish you had, and therefore you find a means to acquire it. I always thought jealousy was silly. I mean, why would one hate someone else for what he/she could have as well? I did envy, however. I still do. I envy celebrities, and their fame and money and influence, but I know that someday I too shall have all of these. But please believe envy alone does not do the trick; you must also be committed through action.

Dealing with jealousy, however, is not so easy. When you find a jealous person—run. Run as far away as possible. Jealous people will tear you down so bad it's not even funny. (The difference between haters and people who are just jealous is that I find jealous people are usually that way sub-consciously, while haters are purposefully malicious. Both, however, can be equally treacherous.) While we are on the subject, let's clear this up. There is no such thing as a jealous friend. Either one is a friend or jealous. How can one appreciate and applaud your achievements, as we have established a friend does, and still criticize and mock them? It's impossible. A friend, however, can become jealous, but at that time he/she is no longer a friend and you must make the choice of either working through it or just distancing yourself. I learned this the hard way. I had a "friend" in high school that always had something negative to say about something I did. If I won an award at school he would say: "OK so what." Soon I realized that he would bring up one of my accomplishments just to joke about it. I know that he did not do it consciously, but I realized that he was jealous. I talk to him to this day, but in no way do I consider him a friend.

7.

Ignorance is Not Bliss But It Is Contagious

If there is one thing that you do not want to be described as, it is being willfully ignorant. I do know what it is, but it is something about an "I don't know and don't care" person that gets under my skin. I mean, even though I'm only 18, I can say that I have met my fair share. I knew a guy in high school that claimed that the KKK was "a reformed organization that sought to do good [for our society]." He then remarked that I was the only one that thought otherwise; mind you I was the only black person in class that day. Then at Morehouse I met someone who held the belief that early blacks were slaves because "they wanted to be." OK sure, these are extreme examples, but that's not all. Ever look at Jay Leno? How about those people on his Jaywalking section who cannot identify President Bush from a picture or sing the first line of national anthem? Or what about the recent statistic that says 13% of the young adults (ages 18-24) in this country could not point out the state in which they lived on a blank map? It's atrocious. When does enough become enough. Where are these people's parents? Better yet, where did they graduate elementary school?

We have all heard that what you do not know will not hurt you. But life shows us otherwise. Look at the prison population; 27% of them claim that they "did not know" that what they were doing was wrong, and another 27% probably did not know the consequences. From SATs to IQ tests even to everyday activities, we realize that those who do not know generally do not succeed. People often quip that Bill Gates "dropped out of college and still became successful," but it is important to note that he was quite knowledgeable in the area of computer science and programming before he ever enrolled in Harvard.

These types of folks are not just ignorant but they generally do not want to change, and that is a problem. Anyone who is blatantly ignorant and is unwillingly to do anything to change that is questionable. They defy our basic human mission, which is to empower ourselves. This type of ignorance is more than a

15

trait but it is an aura, and I have found it is quite contagious. Even if you are already learned, an ignorant person has the ability to rub off on you and cause you to forgo and even despise your education.

So what are the characteristics of a willfully ignorant person? I am glad you asked. Laziness, slothfulness and indolence are all telltale signs. This type of person never seems to know anything, and worse, never attempts to learn anything. This type of person, ironically enough, is dangerous. They are dangerous because they perpetuate the cycle of negativity that is present in our American society today. Remember, ignorance is what breeds racial intolerance, social discrimination, and the like. My advice to you is to distance yourself from them. Do not associate with them in anyway. They obviously do not want to learn from you, for if they did, they would not wallow in their ignorance. Therefore, you must assume that they are probably around you just to bring you down.

President Kennedy, in the wake of the Cuban Missile Crisis, once said: "The best thing to do is make the right decision; the next best thing to do is make the wrong decision; and the worst thing to do is do nothing." Nothing is exactly what blatantly ignorant people do. They do not try to learn or better themselves; instead they laugh and continue in their ignorance. Do yourself and humanity a favor, and do not become one of them. Strive to be knowledgeable because being dumb is neither fun nor profitable. As quiet as is kept, at the end of the day an ignorant person is just ignorant—and that's it.

8.
Don't Boast

If there is one thing you can do to make certain you will have more enemies, go around boasting. Nobody—I repeat nobody—likes a bragger. Remember the guy in school who talked about winning that lousy game of basketball for what seemed like months afterward. Annoying, huh? That is just how you will be perceived if you go around constantly talking about your accomplishments. Its okay to mention them every once in a while, but going on and on about it is a recipe for trouble.

It's unfair I know, but those who are already the object of jealousy of many must be extremely careful not to boast. Just look at it this way: the better your accomplishment, the less you should mention it. Chances are people are already insecure about their position in life and reminding them about your success only adds salt to the wound. This does not mean that you have to downplay it when others bring it up. It helps, however, to appear more modest about it than you actually are; but do not be overly modest or it will backfire. If somebody congratulates you, a simple "thank you" or "I appreciate it" will do; if you have won say something along the lines of "well I could not have done it without you" or "thank you so much for your support" is best. Steer away from responses like "that was a huge trophy wasn't it?" or "he was crazy to run against me anyway", and those overly-modest remarks like "I wasn't even expecting it", "I never thought in a million years they'd pick me", or "no, I really don't deserve it." It's OK to feel like that, but just do not say it. Remember these are tips to being a *successful* person and sometimes that means not sharing everything that comes to mind.

In dealing with boastful people, and believe me you will deal with them, remember the underlying reason for why they brag. Many times they do so to boost their self-esteem. I once had a teacher who did everything and traveled everywhere; let him tell it, he had been around the world numerous times, helped write the course of history, and held company with some of the world's most affluent people—all while holding down a job as the King of England. Yeah right. Some people brag to make others feel smaller about their own accomplish-ments. I knew a guy in high school who would wait for me to tell him something and then counter it with his own exaggerated feat. I would get an award, but that did not matter because he had "gotten" it a year before; I'd run a mile in PE class in 6:30 only for him to say that he had done it a month before in 5:30. Then you have people who brag just because they like to hear themselves talk. But all brag-gers have a common link; they are insecure and they are disliked. Take it from me, do not become one of them.

9.
Keep Your Opinion to Yourself,
Unless Asked

Boy did I learn this one the hard way? I was a know-it-all in high school—or at least I thought I was. No one had to wait to ask me for my two cents worth, because chances are by then I had already given them. If you had failed a test, don't come to me, because I was there to tell you that you "did not study enough." Or even if you were sick I was on hand to let you know it was you who brought it on yourself with your "defeatist attitude." As time went on and I matured, I realized that I was being judgmental and too critical. I am still trying to fully learn this, but now at least I have a better grasp; I know to keep my opinion to myself, unless I am asked.

First I had to realize that my opinion was exactly that, *my* opinion. Everybody has one and nobody's is more significant. No matter how much one tries to see from another's perspective, it is impossible. Just as one can never look through another's eyes, one can never see from another's point of view. Therefore, what you see as the reason for a circumstance or situation can be totally misconstrued as a result of your own folly. This leads to the second thing I had to learn, and that is that I was entirely too scathing. I held everyone to the standard I held myself, as many achievers do, and that was equally wrong. Not everyone has the same drive or motivation. So a C on a report card might be acceptable to someone else's parents and therefore it's not my place to say: "Well my mom would have killed me." Thirdly, I was too rash in giving my judgment. The Bible says it best in Proverbs: "In all your getting, get understanding." I was too quick to give my synopsis, barely before the last word was uttered, if I even waited for the last word. These are all characteristics that will earn you the dreaded title "judgmental."

Here is how I found to avoid it. First of all, listen to the person who is talking. Don't just hear, but listen intently to what they are saying. Wait for them to finish. Ask questions to better understand. Then if they ask, deliver your verdict.

Even then, do not be overly harsh or overly critical. Do not merely tell them what they want to hear, but tell them honestly how you see it, but in a caring way. Afterward talk it through with them. Sometimes you must just agree to disagree and move on. There are some exceptions, however. When dealing with a friend, if you see that it is hurting your relationship, tell him/her how you feel. That is the beauty of friends; they should be readily able to hear your opinion, even if they did not ask, or even want it at the time. But still remember there are levels to friendships and they are people too, so do not just blast into them. Sometimes a simple conversation is the difference between clearing up a misunderstanding and a broken friendship.

10.
It is Both What You Say, and How You Say It

This is yet another thing that I struggle with on a daily basis. Perhaps my best example of this is what happened to me this past year. I was running for class president for the second time and it was the May of 2004. I was campaigning against three other people. The highlight of the race was the debate; it was right on the night before Election Day. I remember it like it was yesterday. The room, which seated about 100 people, was jam packed with about 300. Most of the people there came to see what I was going to say, especially considering I was the front-runner. Boy, did I give them a show. Two questions were for all the candidates and the other two were just for me. I made light of the failures of the incumbent class officers. Our year was terrible and everybody knew it. It was a complete failure and everybody knew that too, but I could not just leave it at that. It did not help that I was more eloquent in speech than probably everyone in that room. To make matters worst the incumbent president and his staff were in the room sitting in the second row. The debate only lasted 10 minutes, but in that short time I had sealed my fate. Many seem to think I would have won the election had I not have been so belligerent. The ironic thing is that I did not really care how bad a job they did; I was saying this because I thought I could play on other people's emotions about it. I made a gross miscalculation.

I learned a life-long lesson in the days following the debate. It was not that people did not believe or even agree with what I said; they did not want to hear it. This brings me to the point that it is both what you say and how you say it that can be offensive. Going back to my example, it's obvious to see how I said it was wrong. I was belligerent and aggressive. I was pointing my finger and waving my fists in a manner that mimicked some infamous Fascist leaders. I used the strongest vocabulary; phrases like "complete failure", "need for leaders who actually lead", and of course my favorite "the game is over" were all a part of it. (Though I never once called the people failures, only their policies, it was implied and equally as hurtful.) This was my delivery, the "how", and in retrospect it was poor. So, let's now focus on the "what" aspect. I disagree with the adage "it's not what you say…" because of this very example. How could I have told the class that their class council had failed them without coming off as offensive? I could not. As much as my delivery hurt me; my message hurt just as much. No matter how much I could have smiled or laughed it off, saying the council was a failure would not have gone over well. Period. This also goes hand in hand with what I said earlier about opinions. Though people wanted to hear mine since I was a candidate, it was entirely too harsh and of course people said I was "judgmental." This in turn leads us to the question of the truth. I was speaking the truth, but the truth does indeed hurt. My message stung not only those who had failed our class, but the ones I was reaching out to for votes, who empathized with them. Do not get me wrong; there were a lot of people who voted for me because they liked my tenacity, but they were outnumbered and hence I lost that election. If I could do it over again, I would not mention the class council at all; therefore I would not have to worry about what I said or how I said it.

I say to you, do not make the same mistake I did. Just be careful, at least until you are in a position to say what you want. Some people are heralded for their candidness and people take it as sincerity; President Bush is a perfect example. Here we have a guy who has grouped together five totally separate nations and called them an "axis of evil", called leaders of unfriendly countries "thugs and evildoers", told Iraqi rebels to "bring it on", called some foreign territories "breeding grounds for terrorists", and then off camera called a reporter a "major league a**hole" and Saddam Hussein a "son of a b**ch". Yet, many of his most loyal fans consider this trait of his a blessing. So until you are around a group of your close friends or you are President of the United States, take my advice and watch what you say to others and how it comes across.

11.
Don't Wait For Validation

One of the fastest ways you stagnate your life and its purpose is to wait for other people's validation. I do not care whether its friends, family or other loved ones. Waiting for others is doing exactly that, waiting (and doing absolutely nothing in the process). George Washington's mom never believed he could make it as a soldier. Wilma Rudolph's doctors never thought she would walk again. And of course there's John Kennedy, who was so sick as a child he was not expected to live past 13. What if they had changed their plans and dreams to better suit those around them?

I will go as far as to say—be grateful that people believe in you, but do not expect it. Most people cannot see the forest for the trees. They are so bogged down by their own problems that they do not have time to assist you in yours. Let's first establish what validation is. It is the approval and blessing, if you will, of one to another. We all want it. As a child you wanted your parents to like your drawings; as a teenager you wanted your peers to accept you as you are; and as an adult you want society to embrace your individuality. OK, that's all perfect in a Utopian world. This is America however. As a child you probably could not draw worth a lick, but your parents put them on the refrigerator anyway because they were yours. As a teenager your peers are going to mostly criticize and pressure you unless of course you just give in and accept mediocrity. Then, as an adult, your individuality means squat, because society has already defined beauty and strength and happiness and talent through Hollywood and the media. So, now it's up to you to do something if you want to be successful.

Encourage yourself. Believe in your own dreams. Tell your closest friends and loved ones. If they approve, cool; if they don't, that's cool too. In the end it's you, not them, who must live up to the decision you made. Besides, it's your life anyway. I know. I know. You are probably saying, well, it's easier said than done. True. I remember telling my dad when I was 15 that I wanted to be the President of the United States; he looked at me and said: "OK, really son, how many black Presidents have there been?" I was distraught to think that my own father would tear down my dreams like that. He did not even give it a second thought, he just said it. But it was my mother who told me that no matter who believed in me, even if it was just myself, I had to go ahead with it. My father is just one of many people who have never been supportive of my dreams and aspirations.

I urge you to get to the point that I am now. I could care less if nobody validates me; my vote of confidence is all I need. Say to yourself that you will be successful and you will achieve everything you set your hands to do, regardless of who likes it. Of course, it helps that my mother is my rock, but for those of you that cannot even turn to home, you have an opportunity to be even more steadfast in yourself. However, I should interject that just because they do not approve of you, does not mean they are against you. Sometimes, in fact, they are not validating you because they think you are making a mistake. Hear them out, but you are the one to make the ultimate decision. Trust in your own judgment. Some, like in the case of my father, are insecure because you are aiming to achieve what they never could. No, you do not have to distance yourself from them, just be careful of what you tell them. Put them on a need to know basis and the fact is they do not need to know what you are aspiring to. Chances are, if they will not validate you, they would probably not support your effort either. Don't sulk about it; just find other means. Be defiant and stubborn in your will to succeed and those who do not approve, well, just brush them off. For those who say that you will not be right or you will not make it, just think to yourself only time can tell.

12.
Accept Full Responsibility for Your Actions

One would think that this rule would go without saying, but it still goes unheeded by many, including those who claim they are striving to be successful. Following this rule you will find will win you the respect of many. Let me say it one more time just in case you forgot it already; accept *full* responsibility for your own actions, all of them.

Ever wonder where those kids are that would pass a lick and then quickly point the finger at someone else? Well, they are all grown-up and now they are on TV—court TV that is. They say things like "she should not have let me borrow her car; she knew I was a bad driver", "I might not have put a leash on my dog, but he still should not have been walking near my yard", and of course the line of so many defendants, "your Honor I promise [the $5000 she gave me after I lost my job] was a gift." This is like a craze sweeping the nation—don't fess up to anything anymore, just pass it off on someone else! Well, it's got to stop; and especially if you plan to be successful, you cannot join the fray.

Hear are a few tips to follow. First, realize that excuses are not valid; their sole purpose is to cover up the one explaining the problem. Do yourself a favor and do not bother with them. When asked what went wrong, start by saying that "there is no excuse for it (sir/ma'am), but I will do my best to correct the problem." You will find by accepting the blame, you will disarm the interrogator and compel them to at least admire you for your straightforwardness. This type of honesty has won many promotions and acclaims. Thomas Edison is the best example. He was part of a group of scientists that invented the light bulb, but two days before they were supposed to present it, he dropped it. He immediately took responsibility and single-handedly rebuilt it. His colleagues were so impressed by this young man's work ethic that they let him present it at the showcase, and today his name graces the history books for it. I must warn you, though, not to get overzealous. If you make a mistake you do not have to run and call someone and fess up if you can correct it without them knowing. If they ask about it later then be honest, but, if they never ask, you do not have to volunteer.

I feel that I must add a clause for all those out there with egos larger than brains: if you are wrong, do everybody a favor and just admit it. Saying you are wrong, and by saying it I mean verbally expressing it to those your actions have negatively affected, takes a lot of honor. But as successful people, you must have it. Therefore swallow your pride and when you are wrong, admit it, and move on. Some people will not forgive you and you cannot change that, but once you make the confession sincerely, it is out of your hands. A simple admission of guilt can be the difference between a short discussion and years of arguing, or worse, resentment. Too many times there are men who cannot say they are wrong, and women who cannot live without them saying it. If you are one of these types of people realize that not saying you are wrong, especially when everybody knows it, does not make you look strong—it makes you look stupid; and if you are the other person who needs someone to say it to move on, get over yourself or that person and stop holding a grudge, because obviously they have moved on with their life.

As you strive for success, you will gain some of the things that come with it: riches, fame, and honor. But to much is given, *more* is required. At all times you are to act in a manner that lets you deserve these treasures. Remember, success cannot be given; it is only earned. You earn it by taking advantage of what you have and doing extraordinary feats with it. You will take chances. Sometimes you will be right, and others you won't be. Whatever the outcome, never ever cower from your mistakes; stand up and take claim. And finally, I say learn. Learn from the mistakes of others; do not repeat them. Learn from the achievements of others, and see how you can do the same.

13.
Your Life is Not a Garbage Can

You have to make up in your mind right now that your life is not a garbage can and you will not let others constantly pour their life's trash into it. OK, let's analyze the situation. You know those people who are always down and out? I mean as soon as they get over their virus, the dog dies; and if they get a new dog, somehow they break their leg playing catch with it. Everything is always going wrong with them, and you are the first one they pick up the phone to tell about it. What about the ones who always complain? I mean always. Their neighbors make too much noise, their bills are too high, the weather is too wet, the house is too small, and of course they have that relative who just keeps getting to them. Whether you realize it or not now, that constant negative talking is affecting you. Just like you seem to feel a little depressed after watching the 6 o'clock news, the same thing is happening. If do not believe me, test it. After you have one of these conversations with somebody, watch how you react. You will be down, and you will keep thinking about the incident and the persons involved. Eventually you will become so occupied with their trouble that you ignore yours and totally lose focus. Wondering if the people you are constantly talking to are like those I just described? You can test that too. Are they always either recovering from something or coming down with something? Are they always fussing about something? Are they saying stuff like "well you remember that darn niece I've been telling you about" or "if it's not one thing it seems to be the other"? Are you always saying stuff like "oh, I am really sorry to hear that", "things will look up eventually", or "please tell me if I can help in any way"? If you find this is the case, you are becoming a trashcan, and this is how to deal with it.

First, you must determine if the person is consciously doing it to distract you. Remember misery really does love company. If they are being malicious, then this person is harmful to your growth as a successful person and therefore you should distance yourself from them. Most times I find that these constant complainers do not do it purposely. However, the end product can be just as dangerous. Therefore, you have to handle it delicately. Tell the person that you find that the conversations you share usually disintegrate into a bash of despondency. If you really want to help the person, tell them that you would like to help them gain a positive outlook on life. If you find the person is unwilling to change, let them be. However, you must lessen the amount of time you spend with them. If the person you are trying to help is making no progress, you must do the same. I know it is much harder to do when it is a loved one, but it is vital to your development. If comes to it, do not pick up the phone or respond to the email. Maybe then they will get the picture.

This goes hand in hand with our discussion on picking the right company because whether you want to admit it, hanging around a constant complainer will eventually cause you to do the same. At all costs you must guard your mind and soul and what you allow to enter it.

So what if you are that person I just mentioned? Well, try to see the brighter side of things and when you do, vocalize that. Instead of talking about how bad the economy is, talk about how grateful you are you have a job. You will find that it eases the atmosphere around you and makes it easier for people to enjoy your presence. Remember that things can always get worse. No matter how much is going wrong in your life, remind yourself that you are still blessed. So, OK, your car is in the shop again, but at least you have one. Finally, look for ways to help those around you. The gift of giving is great in that it helps one to feel good about him/herself. That feeling of self-gratitude makes the small things seem that much smaller.

14.
Age is Nothing but a Number, Take Advantage of your Youth

King Josiah ruled Israel at the height of its early prestige and he was only 8. Alexander the Great conquered an empire that spanned from India to Greece to Egypt and Asia Minor, and he had not even turned 30. And who can forget Martin Luther King, Jr. who led one of the largest civil rights campaigns in modern history while helping found more than 10 groundbreaking organizations and died before seeing his 40th birthday. These are all examples of people who did extraordinary things despite being criticized as being "too young." Being a young adult I have always heard that my opinions will change when I "get some years." And that may well be, but that does not mean that I am not just as much a human being as the next. You can achieve just as much and more if only you put your mind to it. Remember, some of the most successful people in history were young, and by many accounts too young.

If you feel as if you are too young to be successful, remember these words of wisdom. Do not spend time trying to make people feel as if you are not too young, just do it. I was always the young one as people saw it. I graduated high school at 17. Now I am a junior at Morehouse College and I just turned 19. If you find that you too are younger than those around you, look at it like I do. Look at it as everybody else being older and being at a disadvantage. Honestly, I have found that being young has definite advantages. I have the advantage of time, meaning that I have more time to do want I want. I also can learn from the mistakes of those that have gone before me. Being young also means that I appear smarter than I am. At the end of the day I have the pleasure of knowing that I am one up on my peers, simply because of my age. That's what you call turning what could be a negative into a positive.

15.
Have a Sense of Humor

If there is one thing that you can count on to make times easier as your go through life aiming to be successful, it is a good sense of humor. Perhaps that is why politicians always seem to have a joke handy; it keeps them lighthearted even in the most alarming situations. This tip goes hand in hand with our earlier discussion on never letting the public see you sweat. A sense of humor is disarming and can sometimes make all the difference in a crucial situation. Case in point: In March of 1933 Franklin Roosevelt was about to be inaugurated as the next President, having defeated the incumbent Herbert Hoover. The ride to the Capitol in the motorcade was icy by all accounts with neither man saying anything to the other. Finally Roosevelt pointed to one of the buildings they were passing and chided, "Nice steel isn't it?" OK, perhaps that was not enough to get Hoover to like him, but at least it did break some of the tension in the atmosphere.

My advice to you is to do the same. Make a joke, especially when the situation is most tense. Heck, even joke about yourself. Laugh at your mistakes. You will find that you will be much more lighthearted. However, there are still limits. Do not belittle yourself or others, and be just as careful not to be scathing. Dirty jokes, racial jokes, gender jokes are a no-no in public; keep those for friends. Steer away from nationalistic jokes as well, believe me, because there is always a group of people who are "from that country" or "speak that language"; it is OK to boast about America, but sometimes even other Americans get offended from that as well. Just like everything else, there is a time and place for it. I do not suggest funerals, memorial services, or even extremely tense situations. Delivery is also important. Whisper it to a neighbor in a small group setting and you run the risk of people thinking you are rude, or worse talking about them; shout it in a crowded room and risk people calling you obnoxious. Gauge the size of the room and the people in earshot. Remember, the whole point of your sense of humor is to lighten the mood and deflect attention from the situation. Doing so offensively or at inappropriate times can have the opposite result. When all else fails, say it to yourself; sometimes it proves just as effective.

I remember this past year I went on a weeklong retreat with my fellow Bonners' Scholars that became a war of pranks. After the night we doused a room in warm water and baby oil, one of the guys took it especially hard. The next day at lunch he would not even look at me, let alone speak to me. Somehow the rest of us at the table got on the subject of how we pranked them. Recalling the course of events, I looked at him and asked, "So, remember after we doused you with water and you came chasing us into our room and you knocked on the door for like 10 minutes? Did you *really* think we were going to answer it?" Gradually his stony face loosened as he tried to hold back a smile. This technique was especially useful in the weeks following the election. Even as pain and disappointment racked me, I said things like "No, I do not really want the office, I just like running for it", "Hold on a second, I am putting the finishing touches on my pity party invitations", and in response to the question why I thought I lost, I quipped, "Because the other guy got more votes." You might be reading this and thinking none of those jokes are funny, but trust me they work well enough when you want to quickly change the subject without seeming smug or letting on that it bothers you. These are examples of how the right amount of humor at the right time serves its purpose.

Along with having a sense of humor, it always helps to have a positive outlook on things. You should be positive about what the future holds, even if things seem as if they will get worse before they get better. As far as other people go, expect the best. Expect people to like you for who you are. Being optimistic does not mean that you forgo your common sense factor. It also does not mean that you should not protect yourself against negativity. You can open up your heart to other people and allow them to win your trust without being foolhardy. Having this type of optimism makes hard situations seem less discouraging and makes the future look brighter.

16.
Make Yourself Known—and Respected

Of all of my tips, this one might seem to be the vainest, but it works. (Besides, who ever said that being successful does not take a bit of vanity?) Becoming successful means that you have to become recognized and sometimes waiting around for someone to just happen to notice you is not enough. So, this is my advice. In everything you do, become the center of attention. Become the most recognizable person. Make sure that are not easily forgotten. Let your name as well as your face become known among all those who will come in contact with you. Sometimes this can mean that you become more "controversial" than "popular", but remember no publicity is bad publicity, and it all works to the same in the end.

I am Darrell Bennett, Jr., one of the most controversial students on Morehouse's campus. Yes, I lost two elections. Yes, I have a group of people who hate the very mention of my name. Yes, I get nasty phone calls and ugly e-mails. Yes, I have been threatened and criticized and threatened some more. Did I mention I am widely controversial? And through it all, yes, I am *very* happy. I am one of the most known and recognizable persons in my class. Perhaps that is why I was chosen to be Man of the Year. When I walk into a room, I am the center of attention. When I start to speak, people generally listen. When I go somewhere, others follow. And I did it in less than a year.

I did it by following a few simple tips. Always show up at important events. But just being present is not enough to get people to recognize you. Meet as many people as you can. Do not go around like someone who is after something (I made this mistake a few times), but just go around nonchalantly. Introduce yourself with your first and last name, and say it at least twice before you leave them. Shake their hands or make some kind of physical contact. This is all a part of making an impressive first impression. Learn people's names and hometowns, and for college students learn their majors as well. (For my first semester at college, I made myself meet two new people every day.) Once you meet them and chat, get their contact information, and give them yours.

When you are at a seminar, become involved. If they need a volunteer for a demonstration, do it. If they ask for questions or an opinion, you should participate. Do not appear over-eager; instead give the impression of calm and poise. Make your presence known in a room. It is especially hard if you are like me, only being 5'7", but my saving grace has always been my speaking skills. I can speak well enough to cover up what I do not have in height—not to mention I am quite aggressive. I want you to learn the term "passively aggressive". This is what you should be in public. Let your voice be heard and do not be afraid to disagree with others. Remember you can disagree without being disagreeable—whatever that means, ha-ha. Do not appear spineless or timid. When you speak, focus on quality and not quantity; in other words do not bore people, but at the same time make your words count. Do not use vocabulary that you cannot properly pronounce or know the meaning of, and pay close attention to your grammar. Wow, it seems I can do a whole section on speaking alone, but back to becoming the center of attention.

The same goes whether you are at work or in the classroom. Make yourself noticeable by always doing your best. Make your work ethic the talk of bosses and professors alike. Does this mean kiss butt? No, but do an excellent job at whatever you are doing. Follow-up afterwards. Ask the professor if she enjoyed reading your paper; ask the boss if the report you submitted was sufficient. Always seem willing to do more if asked. This makes you appear that much more of a good employee or student, which in turn wins you attention and respect.

17.
Dealing With the Reputation

Applying these techniques will earn you a reputation among both those you know and some you do not. Sometimes you will like it and other times you will not, but either way you are on your way to becoming successful. You notice that people will take notice of you more and listen to what you have to say. Some will respect that and others simply won't. Being the center of attention means that people will form opinions about you before they even meet you; this I find can be the hardest part of it because their first impression, which comes from what they have *heard*, is usually quite hard to change. Remember through all this that not everyone is known, so just having a reputation is an achievement in itself.

Now, once you begin to become known, you will be lumped into one of two categories "controversial" or "popular". Both can be equally advantageous. Being controversial, like I have become at college, means that you generally field strong feelings from others. Your peers will either really like or really dislike you. You will be talked about and joked about, as well as admired and respected. You will have a loyal following, but you will also have many haters. You will have to be that much more careful of how you appear in public, but it will cause you to cherish friendships even more. Being "popular" is what many people want to be. In high school I was "popular". You have less haters and more people who pretend to like you. As a "popular" person you are expected to always be happy and cheerful. Though people will generally have strong feelings toward you, there will be a lot more who will lie about them. In addition, I found in being popular that many feel as if you owe them something.

Having been on both sides, I find that I like being controversial more. It is a lot harder, but I enjoy the challenge. I rather know who is for or against me, than have to constantly guess. But as vain as this might sound, I just enjoy the attention. Most people would, I am just the first to admit I like it. When I sit down and hear people whisper my name and point to me, when I meet a person who says, "boy have I heard about you?" or when I say my name and see the person's expression change, because they already heard it, I feel as if I am that much closer to being successful. I look at it like this, if people are talking, whether good or bad, I must be doing something. Sure, I have had people go out of their way to share a kind word. Sure, some of the things hurt sometimes and I get really mad. But it all pans out at the end of the day.

Here is my advice to you. If you have a reputation, no matter what it is, some people are going to dislike you. I have figured that is just one of the laws of the universe; so do not spend time trying to change the inevitable. However, this does not mean that you cannot strive to be a better person; you must always be willing to search within yourself and build a stronger character.

If you think that it's just as profitable to go through life being unknown, I could not disagree more. Now, you do not have to be known by or know everyone, just the ones that are important to you achieving the purpose for which you were put on this earth. For instance, would Oprah have become who she is had she not had the acclaim of being the first black anchorwoman in the country, or would Kennedy have been so successful had his father not raised him around some of the most affluent people in the nation? They are examples of how being known and building a reputation has proved extremely profitable. Do not fool yourself by thinking you have your whole life to do it. Carpe Diem. Life is now and you must seize your opportunity for success not later, but now—right now.

18.
Do Things That You Enjoy

All work and no play made Jake a very dull boy. Some of America's most successful people are best at just relaxing and vacationing. Ever heard of Martha's Vineyard and the Hamptons? Doing things that you enjoy is essential to your growth and development as a successful person. The alternative is overloading yourself, causing you to burnout. Do not think of it as wasting time; just look at it as recharging your life-batteries.

How often and how much you choose to relax or do things that you enjoy is ultimately your decision. I suggest setting aside at least twice a week for down time. That could be as simple as turning into bed early or sleeping in. If you like sports, spend a morning on the courts, on the field, or even working out; you will find that you will go through the day refreshed. I enjoy movies; last semester I went to the local theatre with my friends every Saturday and I found that to be quite rewarding. I used to play chess to relax, but I found that I would be so concentrated on the game that it defeated the purpose. Relaxing means that your mind is not just diverted from its everyday problems, but it is actually calmed. I was never a sports fanatic to say the least; I know it's kind of sad, but I actually find trying to hit the ball or making the basket is more stressful than it is fun. My best friend played baseball in high school and I found that even watching the game was stressful. Ha-ha. Like I say, to each his own.

Hanging out with friends is essential to relaxing. It is proven that having company improves morale. As you strive to become successful, you will find that your friends, who are true and trustworthy, will become fewer and fewer in number. You will learn to cherish and appreciate their friendship more and more. Enjoy your time with them. This is your time to just have fun without worrying about how you appear or what people think. Remember, it's not often that you can be totally open, so be grateful for the times you can.

19.
Plan For the Future

One of the biggest mistakes you can make on your journey to becoming success-ful is not planning for the future. Notice, I say plan for the future and not for *your* future, because no one knows what his or her future holds. However, there are preparations that you can make to ensure that as time passes, you stay the course to obtaining and continuing your success.

First and foremost, you must have a plan. When I say plan, I mean a written plan; no, having an idea in your head is not enough. Write a list of short-term goals (benchmarks of success that you would like to reach in the next couple of months), and a list of long-term goals (benchmarks that you would like to reach in the distant future). The lists should read in descending order of priority. Under each item you should write the essentials: what it takes to reach it, who will be involved, how fast you can do it, and of course how much it costs. Then sketch a broad outline that includes all of the goals. I know it is a bit of work, but this is your life. Now, remember that the theme of your plans should be effi-ciency, meaning cost and time conscious. Do not "give" yourself longer than it takes to complete a goal; that begets laziness. Do not put things like "go on diet" on the outline either; if you know you need to go on a diet, just go on a diet now. Since you can add to the outline as you go along, do not get overzealous and include goals like "buy the $75,000 tennis bracelet." Remember, this is not a dream list or even a budget; this is a list of goals you are actively working towards in order to become a successful individual. This does not mean that you cannot be optimistic, but a tennis bracelet, for instance, is a possible result of your suc-cess, not a means to it.

Along with your goals and outline include a segment where you describe your ideal self. Now write out your dreams. If you want to be famous, write about yourself as a famous person; if you want to be wealthy, write about what you would like to do with that wealth. In this segment it helps to use a person as your gauge. This person is someone who is currently where you would like to be, sort of like a role model. For me that person is President Clinton. OK, now I know I won't be a white man, but I can be the President of the US and live my life as a statesman doing good for people all over the world. I also choose Clinton because his background is similar to mine and his story gives me hope that I too can live the American Dream. Your person might be deceased, or a relative.

Once you have compiled this plan; make sure that you look at it at least once a week. Unless you feel compelled, there is no need to share it with anyone. Make revisions and changes as needed to add, but hopefully never to delete, goals. Keep it somewhere safe like in a Bible or in a chest. Most of all cherish it and look forward to what the future holds.

20.
Learn From Other's Example

This is perhaps one of the most important principles to pursuing success in life. No matter how bogus the situation, someone else has already gone through it, and learning from their experience can sometimes be the difference between boom and bust. Some people would argue that each person has to go through life experiencing everything for themselves in order to learn. I totally disagree.

In life we are given three types of examples to follow, the first being relational. For instance, my maternal great-grandmother got pregnant young, out-of-wedlock, and with a man who soon left her and the baby. The trend continued to my mother, who got pregnant with me when she was 21 with my father who left us soon after. My mother tells me to this day that had she truly learned, and not just listened, to her mother's experience, things might have been different. Relational examples sometimes turn into trends following generations through the centuries. The second type of example is a human example. This example comes from a person, either living or dead, who has carved an image for themselves that will live on in history in generations to come. More than just storybooks that should be read on Sunday mornings, the ultimate purpose of religious books, like the Bible, is to present people and their situations to provide examples for life today. King David is known for his benevolence in ruling ancient Israel, but he is also symbolizes what God's judgment can be, as he saw first-hand when he slept with Bathsheba. Paul is hailed for being the greatest missionary of the Church, but he is also an example of how strong and compelling God's grace is. Other examples are not in the Bible, yet they hold their own place in history. Napoleon ruled all of Europe at the height of his power, but he fell in his march east, becoming the classic example of the consequences of greed. Theodore Roosevelt lost his beloved wife to child-birth early in his career, so he left home, entered politics and eventually became one of the greatest leaders in American history, becoming the representation of how a bad situation can be turned around for good. The third and perhaps most compelling type of examples are myths. They didn't happen as they are told, but they are true because their message is timeless. We were taught them at a young age in order to shape our character. Humpty Dumpy was careless. Cinderella was beautiful, despite her step-mother's brooding. Jack and Jill were inseparable friends. But they all had a story.

My advice to you is learn from others. With learning comes listening. I had this problem; I loved to talk, but I rarely listened. Listen to what others have to say, even if you disagree with them, because in the end you decide whether to use it. Understand what they did and how it ended up the way it did—whether good or bad. If it was good learn how you can employ it, but if it was bad, steer clear of it. If it happened to someone else, will it happen to you? Not necessarily; however, it is important to note that insanity is doing the same thing expecting different results. Let me interject here. If you are expressing an idea and someone else is breaking their neck to tell you about their negative example, chances are they are doing so to dishearten you. Do not say, "Well that will not happen to me" or "that was your experience," because that will only inflame the situation. Instead, say something along the lines of "only time will tell." Of course if you believe in yourself go ahead with that restaurant business, even if everybody else you know failed, but do not do *exactly* what they did—improve. Do not fall into the same ditches as someone else if you can help it. This shows the importance of educating yourself. Read the biographies and autobiographies of those who have succeeded in what you are striving for; then read the ones of those who did not. Learn from what these people did and then determine how best to pursue your goals. Remember, if you are blind, you do not need another one leading you to into a ditch; chances are you will do it on your own.

21.
Think Big

In elementary school we had a song that went like this:

Big. Big. Big. Big.
I might as well think big.
Why should any thoughts be small?
I might as well think big—
If I'm going to think at all.

This is the attitude that I encourage you to adopt. In everything you do, think large-scale. This does not mean that you are unrealistic. As a matter of fact, let's examine the difference between thinking big and being unrealistic. Thinking big is believing for the extraordinary in your life. Being unrealistic is believing for the extraordinary in your life, but not working to see it realized. William Blythe IV was thinking big when he told an elementary school teacher that he wanted to be President of the United States. From then to Georgetown to Rhodes to Yale to being Governor, he worked diligently to see it realized and on January 1993 he, William Jefferson Clinton, became the 42nd President. I have a friend who was unrealistic when he told me in middle school that he wanted to run track and field in the 2004 Summer Olympics. He quit the track team; he ran twice a week; and to top it off he had not even run a district meet in two years. These are two different men with two extraordinary goals, but two very different outcomes. This leads me to believe that there are three types of people in the world: big thinkers, surrealists, and then the saddest, those who do not even dare to dream.

Think big and dream for the extraordinary, regardless of what people might say. Sometimes thinking big means that it defies the status quo, which means that instead of following in someone else's trail you may have to blaze your own. In whatever you aim to be, strive to be the best and most respected in that field. Most people can only think as big as they see; only few and far between think even bigger. Even now, when I watch shows like MTV Cribs I am amazed by how big some of the houses are, but no matter how big they are I have already imagined it. The problem, as we said earlier, is not working actively and diligently to see your goals realized. Your dreams and goals should *never* exceed your work ethic. If they do, you do not have to scale your dreams, just step up your effort. Make it so that what you are doing to see your goals realized matches the scale of your goals. And since we are striving to be successful, then all our goals should be big. (By goals, I mean long-term.) Remember, successful people are successful, because they expect, and many times, demand extraordinary effort of themselves in their everyday life.

Like everything else, there is a rule to this principle, and that is keeping silent. In other words think as big as you want, but keep your thoughts just that, *your* thoughts. Sure, you can tell your closest friends and family, but it is best left at that. Remember, success scares people, but more importantly it intimidates them. It is easy to make enemies and obtain haters just by going around telling people how great a person you *want* to be. In addition, people will challenge to you and the "realistic"-ness of your dreams. These types of situations and people only make things worse for you, and can in no way benefit you. Therefore, it is best that you keep your thoughts to yourself, even when asked. Remember, having people disagree or agree with your goals will not make them anymore feasible, only your work ethic can do that.

22.
Avoid the Appearance of Wrongdoing

In this book we talk a lot about appearance versus reality, but perhaps the best piece of advice I can give on this subject is avoid even looking wrong. Last year a poll taken among police officers showed that 42% of the time a pull-over or questioning is prompted because the person "looked suspicious"; however it only led to arrest in 8% of those cases. It is astonishing how many times we are profiled in life solely based on how our actions "appeared".

Appearance is made up of three basic components: company, attire and actions. This is why we established early on the importance of picking the right company; you can easily look like something just based on the people you are around. Remember those cliques we talked about? You may not know Bob, for instance, but you would assume that he does drugs just because the group he hangs with does drugs. Is this assumption wrong? It might be, but the question here is not right/wrong, it is appearance/reality; and whether Bobs likes it or not he "looks" like a drug user. The second component is attire. I am a firm a believer that dress can make all the difference. Whether you are willing to admit it or not, I am sure you believe the same. Case in point, take a man about 21 dressed in baggy jeans, a long white tee-shirt and a skull cap—harmless enough, right? Well, take that same man in a high-end luxury store. Hmmm, sounds suspicious right? You may not think so, but it is enough to cause a security guard to follow him through the aisles. Is that right? Not necessarily, but he is being profiled negatively solely based on how he looks. The third and most important component of your appearance is your actions. What you do or say most concisely speaks of your character, or at least that is the consensus. Remember that African man in New York shot 41 times because police thought he was "reaching for a gun", but in actuality he was getting his wallet? Did you buy it? I surely didn't, but that is a different conversation. Anyway, whether they believed it or not, they used the defense that his actions were questionable to justify theirs.

My mother once told me "Somebody is *always* watching." And so far her intuition has proved true. Most times people are caught doing wrong when they thought nobody was around. Therefore, it is important to build your character. Do good deeds for the sake of it, not for who's watching or for the reward. If you make a habit of doing good, then you will not have to worry as much about doing things that are questionable. As a person striving for success your character must be beyond reproach, meaning that no one can cast a shadow of a doubt on your honor and decency. Most people are not concerned with whether one is right or wrong, sadly enough; they judge others on how the situation looks. In order to protect yourself, ask yourself these questions. Does this look wrong? What would I think? Are people I care about going to think differently of me for this? If you can yes to any of the above, then you should probably just find another activity. However, remember that people are *always* going to talk and someone will *always* misconstrue or cast doubt on your motives. Do not worry about them; rather set your sights on shielding your character and its moral fiber.

23.
Practice the Art of Giving

Oprah Winfrey. John Rockefeller. Andrew Carnegie. And did I mention Oprah Winfrey. These are all people who made the gift of giving an art, a lifestyle, and for it they have won the respect of the world. Growing up I was always told by my elders that a person was blessed to be a blessing. Now I know first-hand what they mean and what it can do.

There are essentially two ways a person can give of himself or herself: time and talents. Giving of one's time includes volunteering, going on mission trips, and taking on projects. Giving of one's talents includes giving money, gifts or other material things. Those who give of themselves, either time or talent, in large amounts is called a philanthropist; the world's most famous is of course Oprah Winfrey. As a child she lived in a home without running water or electricity in one of the poorest sections of Chicago, now she is a billionaire who owns a media conglomeration that grosses over $80 million a year. Oddly enough, she did it by giving. Yes, she became wealthy by giving money away. With the Angel Network and other such organizations, she has managed to give away over $300 million since she first entered the business. Like Rockefeller, who said since he was a small boy he was taught that a "dime from every dollar" was to be given away, she made her giving a way of life. In doing so she has earned respect and success in every region of the world.

You can do the same if you adopt their mindset. Look for ways *you* can better other's lives. Do not just talk about it. Consider your blessings and see how you can use them to help your fellow man. If are a poet, for instance, write poems to loved ones to lift their spirit. If you are good in math, maybe find someone that you know is struggling and help him get better. Instead of boasting about your talents, share them. At the same time, you should not feel bad for being blessed. (I have found that most times people feel "guilty" about their achievements, because they are *not* helping someone else with them.) In order to have a giving heart, you cannot be stingy; a stingy person selfishly withholds that which could be used for good to benefit only themselves.

Tip well. Give to DAV and the Salvation Army. Leave money in foundation collection boxes. Put pennies in the jar in front of the cash register. Tutor others if they are willing to learn. Help walk someone across the street if they ask. These are all ways of getting in the habit of giving of yourself.

But why? Why give away time or talents if the goal is for *me* to be successful? This is an excellent question and more frequently asked than one would think. Remember, we said that giving is a lifestyle and therefore a mindset. Successful people see giving as a means to obtain, not as a waste; that is why we say giving *of*, not *away*. When you give of your time and talents, you are essentially finding your sense of self and bringing out your best quality. Those who do not give, never find a sense of true self, because instead of sharing and enhancing their skills, they hide and hoard them. In essence, you have to look at it like stocks. When you buy stocks you invest money in someone else's company; like when you give, you are investing into someone else's future. In return, and sometimes much later, you may grow financially, because the value of your shares increases and so does your interest in the company; just as the person you are helping may be fruitful and even bless you in return. But there is a risk; stocks, like the person or project you are devoted to, might fail and instead of gaining wealth you might only gain wisdom. The alternative is being stingy and holding on to everything you have been blessed with, or in the financial sense sticking your money in a hole in the wall. Sure, there is no risk, but there is absolutely no room to gain either wisdom or wealth—both of which are crucial on your road to becoming successful.

24.
Exhibit Self-Discipline

In order to achieve success and become a person who is worthy of it, you must be in control of your body—mentally, physically and psychologically. Because the amount of control you will have over your surroundings varies, you must focus on practicing self-discipline. Your actions and your behavior are an extension of your attitude and personality. Therefore, you must spend time fine-tuning them.

First of all learn to tame your tongue. It is so small, yet it can do so much damage. Be cautious in your judgments, timely in your praise, and constructive in your criticisms. Steer away from petty arguments. An argument should only occur when you feel that agreeing to disagree is not enough and the issue at hand must be resolved. If you are like me and love to debate, choose the time wisely. Do not take everything so personally. If you feel you are being attacked, analyze why. Remember, the haters do not dislike you just because they have nothing else to do; they dislike you because you are achieving what they want. Therefore, do not pay them any attention; do not even give them the satisfaction of an evil glare. Ignore ignorance and blatantly ignorant people, especially if you find it makes you mad. Only you know what makes you angry; steer clear of those situations. As much as you can help it, do not give in to taunts or feed negativity. Never let your emotions rule you; think rationally through situations. When in doubt, do not say anything at all, and if you are still upset, leave the situation and deal with it later. Do not fly off the handle. Let me repeat that for those out there who have horrible temper problems. It is *never* OK to just fly off the handle. My father has a horrible temper problem and it has caused him endless problems. I inherited this, but my mother worked me through it early on; even still sometimes I feel it resurfacing, but I quell it quite quickly. The truth is that somebody always has control over you: either you or the person that you allow to make you "lose your cool." A person who maintains self-discipline even in the toughest situations is bound to win the respect of friends and foes alike. He/she can be entrusted to think rationally and make solid judgments, just as a person striving for success should.

Now that we have talked about mental and psychological self-control, let's talk about maintaining and disciplining your physical body. This is just as important, because if your body shuts down, you will not be doing much of anything. Develop a consistent sleep pattern and stick with it. You should not be regularly sleeping into the afternoon; that is slothfulness. Think of your body as an engine that demands the best fuel to be at its optimum state. Eat healthy meals. Regularly consume fruits and vegetables, and drink plenty of water. Fast food should be a treat, not a habit. Steer away from fatty, oily foods. Being in college has proved especially hard for me to have the proper diet, but I still try my best. Finally, I suggest exercise. Do some types of cardiovascular work once a week at least. It's not necessary to go to a gym, jogging around the neighborhood and swimming in the neighborhood pool is quite sufficient. Remember, in doing these things, that having a tip-top body is part of living out a long prosperous life as a successful man or woman.

25.
Keep the Faith and Stay the Course

This can be the hardest thing to do when you are striving to be successful and everything around you is going haywire. But you must keep the faith. Sometimes you are the only person who will believe in you, but like I said earlier your vote of confidence is all that matters. Stay steadfast in your goals and your will to succeed.

After losing this past election, I felt hopeless. I began to doubt my talents and myself. I began to wonder if I could even make it as a politician if I could not even win a college election. But then I had to encourage myself. I had to say to myself that I would be successful and that I would continue striving for excellence, even if I lost every election I went up for. Abraham Lincoln lost several major elections before he became Illinois' senator and later one of the most celebrated Presidents in our history. George W. Bush lost a congressional election just two years before he became Governor of Texas, the only person to win two consecutive elections as chief executive of that state. Donald Trump went bankrupt before he became a billionaire. Oprah got fired from her first major job as an anchorwoman before hosting, producing and owning the Oprah Winfrey Show, which has been #1 for the past 10 years.

Society places limitations on us that we call deformities. I call them chances to beat the odds. Moses stuttered, yet he led one of the most celebrated liberations in the history of man. Beethoven could not hear, yet he composed some of the most beautiful and famous music pieces of the past millennium. Franklin Roosevelt could not walk, yet he led the free world during the bloodiest war of all time. History has proven time and time again that we can do incredible things, but first we have to believe in ourselves.

I am proud to say that I am now more confident than ever, and I hope reading this book will make you feel the same. You do not have time to sit around and have a pity party about all the things that you do not have. You have to preserve and fight. No; life is not fair and it never will be, but it's up to you to control your destiny. Never quit. Never give up. Never give in. If you fall, get up again. Have that same positive outlook that people like Gandhi and Mother Teresa had. If you believe in God, continue to believe in Him despite the nay-sayers. But most of all, believe in your power as an individual. Have faith that what you do can change society for the better. Have faith that you control your actions. Be like a child and never stop believing in the impossible. Realize that with the right amount of work and intensity, you can achieve whatever level of success you want. Remind yourself each day that you—yes you—are the future and your development into a successful individual begins right now!

The Challenge

These are just 25 of the tips I found most important to attaining success. I am not an expert—nobody is; I am just another person who wanted to do his share in our world. I want to thank you for reading this entire book and I hope it speaks to your innermost being. I truly do hope that it was as pleasurable for you reading it, as it was for me writing it. Although I geared it to the aspiring young adult, these tips can prove equally beneficial to anyone who heeds them.

In closing I leave you with this challenge. Now that you have read; it is your turn to apply it. Read it as many times as you need and discuss it with friends and family. Write your plan for the future and begin to enact it. Help others along the way and be a blessing to loved ones. Make up in your mind that you will be successful and let nothing hinder you. In all that you do, remember Robert Kennedy's famous quote, "Some people look at things as they are and say 'why'; I dream of things that never were and ask 'why not'?"

Dare to be different. Dare to think big and work hard. Dare to aspire to accomplish the impossible and defy the odds. Dare to be unique and deal with whatever criticism that follows. Dare to exceed the status quo and reach the stars. Dare to make stumbling blocks your stepping-stones. Dare to believe in yourself and your talents even when you are the only one. Dare to be great and break the barriers that society places. Dare to stand in the face of adversity and laugh. Dare to hope, to dream, to aspire and then to achieve.

And I guarantee you—your life will *never* be the same.

0-595-32459-2

Printed in the United States
214498BV00001B/4/A